Math in Focus

Singapore Math
by Marshall Cavendish

2B

Enrichment

Consultant and Author
Dr. Fong Ho Kheong

Author
Ang Kok Cheng

Marshall Cavendish
Education

US Distributor

Houghton
Mifflin
Harcourt

COMMON
CORE

© Copyright 2009, 2013 Edition Marshall Cavendish International (Singapore) Private Limited

Published by Marshall Cavendish Education
Times Centre, 1 New Industrial Road, Singapore 536196
Customer Service Hotline: (65) 6213 9688
US Office Tel: (1-914) 332 8888 | Fax: (1-914) 332 8882
E-mail: cs@mceducation.com
Website: www.mceducation.com

Distributed by
Houghton Mifflin Harcourt
222 Berkeley Street
Boston, MA 02116
Tel: 617-351-5000
Website: www.hmheducation.com/mathinfocus

First published 2009
2013 Edition

Marshall Cavendish® and *Math in Focus*® are registered trademarks of Times Publishing Limited.

Singapore Math® is a trademark of Singapore Math Inc.® and Marshall Cavendish Education Pte Ltd.

Math in Focus® Enrichment 2B
ISBN 978-0-669-01581-2

Printed in Canada

5 6 7 8   1401   23 22 21
4500842059   A B C D E

Contents

Introducing

Math in Focus®

Enrichment

Written to complement *Math in Focus®: Singapore Math by Marshall Cavendish* Grade 2, exercises in *Enrichment 2A* and *2B* are designed for advanced students seeking a challenge beyond the exercises and questions in the Student Books and Workbooks.

These exercises require children to draw on their fundamental mathematical understanding as well as recently acquired concepts and skills, combining problem-solving strategies with critical thinking skills.

Critical thinking skills enhanced by working on *Enrichment* exercises include classifying, comparing, sequencing, analyzing parts and whole, identifying patterns and relationships, induction (from specific to general), deduction (from general to specific), and spatial visualization.

One set of problems is provided for each chapter, to be assigned after the chapter has been completed. *Enrichment* exercises can be assigned while other students are working on the Chapter Review/Test, or while the class is working on subsequent chapters.

BLANK

Mental Math and Estimation

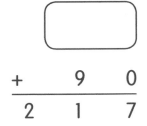

PROBLEM SOLVING
Thinking Skills

Solve.
Show your work.

1. Find the missing number in the sum below.

```
      ┌─────────┐
      │         │
      └─────────┘
  +   9   0
 ────────────
  2   1   7
```

2. What is the difference between 645 and the sum of 195 and 5?

3.   Estimate the numbers at points A and B to the nearest 10.
Then, find their sum.

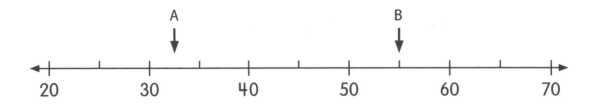

4.   A ticket to the fair costs $17 for an adult.
A ticket for a child costs $8.
Estimate the total cost of tickets for 2 adults and 3 children.

The total cost of tickets for 2 adults and 3 children is about

$_____.

PROBLEM SOLVING
Strategies

Solve.
Show your work.

5.   Justin and David took part in a math contest.
     Justin scored 8 points.
     David scored 10 points more than Justin.
     How many points did they score as a team?

     Justin and David scored _____ as a team.

6.   A pair of pants costs $17.
     A shirt costs $8 less than a pair of pants.
     Estimate the total cost of a shirt and a pair of pants.

     A shirt and a pair of pants cost about $_____.

7. Mia bought a book three weeks ago.
She read 30 pages in the first week.
She read 60 pages in the second week.
She read the remaining 25 pages in the third week.
How many pages are there in the book?

There are _____ pages in the book.

8. There are now 10 apples and 10 oranges in a basket.
Peter had replaced 8 apples with 7 oranges.
How many apples and oranges in all were in the
basket at first?

There were _____ apples and oranges in all at first.

Solve mentally.

9. 115 − 114 + 113 − 112 + 111 − 110 + 109 − 108

PROBLEM SOLVING

Exploration

10. Use at least 2 methods to find the sum of 160 and 80.

11. Use at least 2 methods to find the difference between 540 and 70.

Journal Writing

Write the steps used to find the sum or difference.

12. $137 + 8 =$ _____

     Step 1 _____

     Step 2 _____

13. $129 + 7 =$ _____

     Step 1 _____

     Step 2 _____

14. $234 - 6 =$ _____

     Step 1 _____

     Step 2 _____

15. $462 - 9 =$ _____

     Step 1 _____

     Step 2 _____

Explain how to find the greatest and the least number that can be rounded to

16.   80

17.   460

CHAPTER 11 Money

PROBLEM SOLVING
Thinking Skills

Solve.
Show your work.

1. Ethan has $15.
   He goes to Mr. Ryan's store to buy 3 items.
   Which 3 items can Ethan buy with his $15?

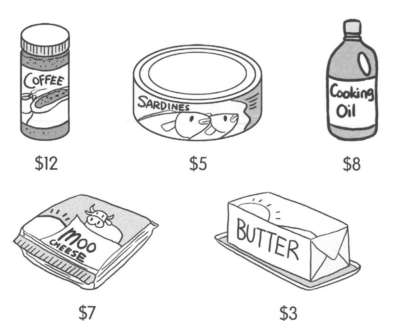

$12 $5 $8

$7 $3

Ethan can buy _____

_____.

Solve.
Use the bar model to help you.

2.   Megan had $103.
She bought a new watch.
She also spent $26 on a bag and $17 on a belt.
She has $7 left.
How much did the watch cost?

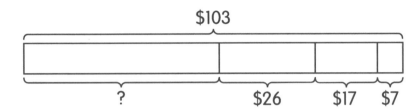

The watch cost $_____.

PROBLEM SOLVING

Strategies

Complete the pattern.
Fill in the missing amounts of money.

3.

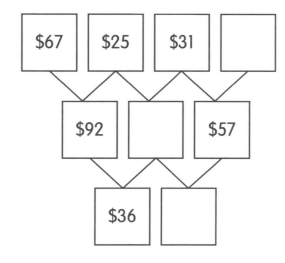

Solve.
Draw bar models to help you.

4. Vera saved $260.
    Mason saved $58 less than Vera.
    Kelly saved $100 more than Mason.
    How much did they save in all?

They saved $_____ in all.

5. Elle has some money.
If she buys 2 comic books, she will have $7 left.
If she buys 3 comic books, she will need $8 more.
How much does each comic book cost?

Each comic book costs $_____.

6. A box of yogurt bars costs $5.
Jacob bought 5 boxes of yogurt bars.
How much money did Jacob spend in all?

Jacob spent $_____.

Name: _____   Date: _____

7.   Eugene bought 2 model cars for $11 each.
He bought 4 pens for a total of $3.
How much money did Eugene spend in all?

Eugene spent $_____.

Each ◯ stands for the same number.

Each ☐ stands for another number.

Find the number that the ◯ stands for.

8.   ◯ + ☐ + ☐ = $450

◯ + ◯ + ☐ = $300

◯ = $_____

PROBLEM SOLVING

Exploration

Solve.
Show your work.

9.   Nathan has a $20 bill.
He asks the cashier to change the $20 dollar bill to smaller bills.
Show 3 ways of changing the $20 bill to smaller bills.

10. Caroline has a $10 bill.
She wants to buy some of these items.

teddy bear   vase   book

$3 $2.25 $6

pencil case   pack of envelopes

$1.50 $2.50

a. Which items can Caroline buy if she wants to buy the greatest number of items?

Caroline can buy _____

_____

b. Which items can Caroline buy if she wants to buy the least number of items and still spend as much of her money as possible?

Caroline can buy _____

_____

Journal Writing

Compare the amounts of money.
Explain the steps used to compare the amounts.
Then fill in the blanks.

11.

Dollars	Cents
45	65

Dollars	Cents
45	30

Step 1 _____

_____

_____

Step 2 _____

_____

_____

So, $_____ is less than $_____.

Write a real-world problem using the words and numbers.
Use the bar model to help you.

12.

Ryan	buys	$550	$192
cost	new suit	left	How much

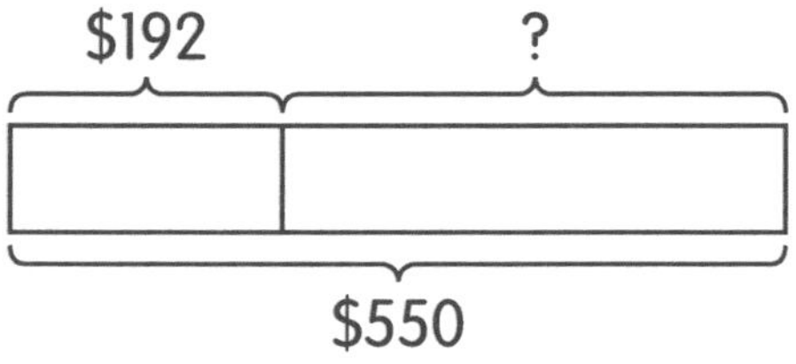

$192   ?

$550

_____

_____

_____

_____

_____

_____

12 Fractions

PROBLEM SOLVING
Thinking Skills

Solve.
Show your work.

1. Divide each square into 4 equal parts.

    Each part is $\frac{1}{4}$.

    There are 4 ways of doing it.

2. Divide each rectangle into 2 equal parts.

    Each part is $\frac{1}{2}$.

    There are 4 ways of doing it.

Shade the part(s) in each model to show the fractions.
Then arrange the fractions from greatest to least.

3. $\frac{1}{2}$

4. $\frac{1}{4}$

5. $\frac{1}{8}$

_____

greatest   least

Shade the parts in each model to show the fractions.
Then arrange the fractions from greatest to least.

6.

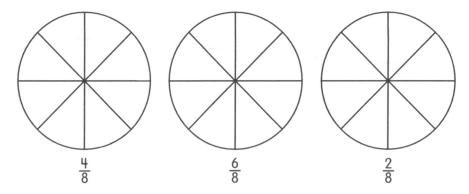

$\frac{4}{8}$ $\frac{6}{8}$ $\frac{2}{8}$

_____

greatest   least

Solve.
Show your work.

7.   Sydney orders a pizza.

She cuts $\frac{2}{9}$ of it for Logan and $\frac{4}{9}$ of it for David.

She eats the rest of the pizza.

What fraction of the pizza does Sydney eat?

Sydney eats _____ of the pizza.

Strategies

Solve.
Show your work.
Fill in the missing fraction.

8.

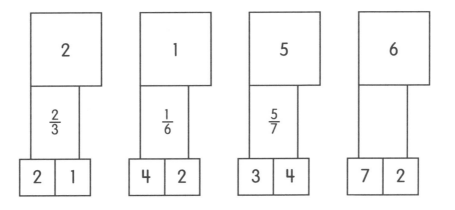

9.   Calvin has a box of crayons.
      He gives 5 crayons to his brother.
      He gives 2 crayons to his friend Tim.
      He gives 3 crayons to his sister.
      He has 2 crayons left.
      What fraction of the crayons does Calvin have left?

      Calvin has _____ of the crayons left.

10. Ava has $\frac{11}{12}$ of a loaf of bread.

Hailey has the rest of the bread.

What fraction of the bread must Ava give to Hailey so that they both have the same amount of bread?

Ava
Hailey

Ava must give _____ of the bread to Hailey.

PROBLEM SOLVING

Exploration

Solve.
Show your work.

11. This set of fractions forms a pattern.
    Describe the pattern.

    $\frac{1}{2}$ $\frac{1}{4}$ $\frac{1}{8}$ $\frac{1}{16}$

    _____

    _____

12. Starting with the fraction $\frac{1}{3}$, write 3 more fractions to form
    a pattern.
    Follow the same rule shown in Exercise 11.

    $\frac{1}{3}$

Journal Writing

Solve and explain.

13. 4 is less than 5.

So, $\frac{1}{4}$ is less than $\frac{1}{5}$.

Explain why this statement is not correct.

_____

_____

_____

_____.

14. The diagram shows $\frac{5}{6}$.

Explain how to find half of $\frac{5}{6}$ with another diagram.

_____

_____

_____

_____.

CHAPTER 13 Customary Measurement of Length

PROBLEM SOLVING
Thinking Skills

Solve.
Show your work.

1. Kenny jumped a distance of 49 inches.
    Kenny and Jim jumped a total distance of 87 inches.
    How much farther than Jim did Kenny jump?

    Kenny jumped _____ inches farther than Jim.

2.   What is the total length of the objects that are less than 30 inches long?

Object	Length (inches)
bookshelf	19
bulletin board	38
ruler	12
pencil case	7

Use the picture to answer the questions.

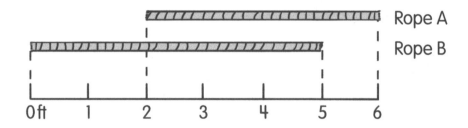

3.   What is the length of Rope B? _____ ft

4.   Which is shorter, Rope A or Rope B? Rope _____

5.   How much shorter is it? _____ ft

6.   What is the total length of Rope A and Rope B? _____ ft

PROBLEM SOLVING
Strategies

Fill in the blanks.

7.   3 ft, 6 ft, _____, 24 ft, 48 ft, _____, 192 ft

Solve.
Show your work.

8.   A pole was painted red and blue.
7 of these poles were lined up one after another.
How long is the line of poles?

	3 ft	2 ft	3 ft	2 ft
Pole	Red	Blue	Red	Blue

The line of poles is _____ feet long.

9. String A is 18 inches long.
String A is 15 inches shorter than String B.
String C is half the length of String A.
What is the total length of String B and String C?

The total length of String B and String C is _____ inches.

10. Grandma Lucille bought some cloth.
She used 7 feet to make a table cloth.
She used 25 feet to make curtains.
She used 6 feet to make a bag.
She has 18 feet of cloth left.
How much cloth did Grandma Lucille buy at first?

Grandma Lucille bought _____ feet of cloth.

PROBLEM SOLVING
Exploration

11. Use a ruler to find the length of some of your friends' shoes.
     Record the data in the table below.
     Then answer the questions.

Friend	Length of Shoe

Who has the longest shoe?
What is the length of the shoe?
Who has the shortest shoe?
What is the length of the shoe?

12. Use a ruler to find the length and width of some of your friends' palms.
Record the data in the table.

Friend	Length of Palm	Width of Palm

Look at the three columns.
Does the widest hand also have the greatest length?

 **Journal Writing**

13. Write the steps used to find the length of the pencil.

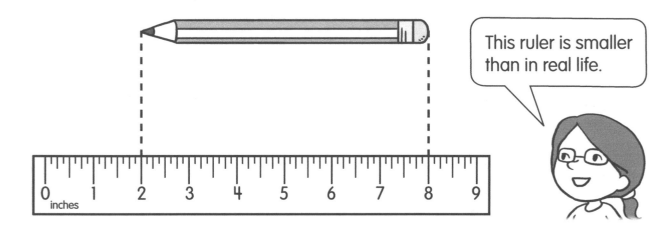

This ruler is smaller than in real life.

Step 1 _____

_____

_____.

Step 2 _____

_____

_____.

14. Write a real-world problem using the following words and numbers.

Mike	Larry	Melvin	5 inches	95 inches	as tall as
twice	taller than	total height	Find	height	tallest boy

_____

_____

_____

_____

_____

_____.

14 Time

PROBLEM SOLVING
Thinking Skills

Answer the question.

1.   Gillian's clock is 15 minutes fast.
      What is the actual time now?

Gillian's clock   _____ P.M.

Draw the hands on the clock.

2.   Jose is going to school 2 hours after 2:30 P.M.

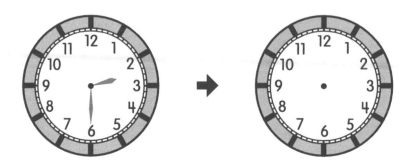

3. Jacob is meeting his friend twenty-five minutes before 7 P.M.

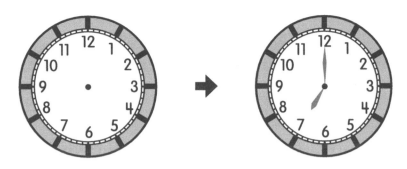

4.

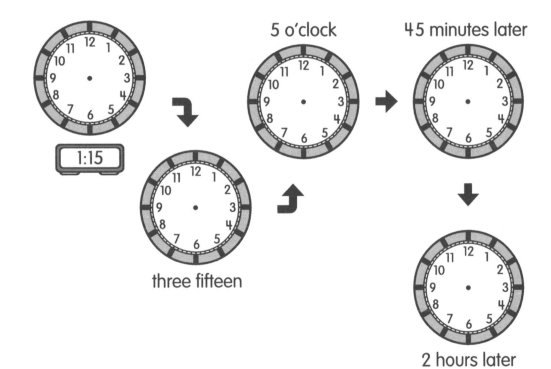

1:15

three fifteen

5 o'clock

45 minutes later

2 hours later

PROBLEM SOLVING
Strategies

Complete.

5.   The times shown on the five digital clocks form a pattern.
       Find the pattern.
       Fill in the time on the last digital clock.

[2:50] [2:55] [3:05] [3:20] [   ]

Solve.
Show your work.

6.   A printer takes 30 minutes to print a banner and a poster.
       It will take 50 minutes to print a banner and three posters.
       How long does it take to print a banner?

       It takes _____ minutes to print a banner.

7.   Peter took 36 minutes to draw a picture of his family.
Kenny took 28 minutes less than Peter.
Sandy took twice as long as Kenny.
How long did Sandy take to draw a picture of his family?

Sandy took _____ minutes to draw a picture.

Solve.
Use the clocks to help you.

8.   Kent left his house to deliver a package to his aunt's house.
It took him 30 minutes to reach his aunt's apartment.
It took another 45 minutes for Kent to get back home.
He got home at 4:15 P.M.
What time did Kent leave his house?

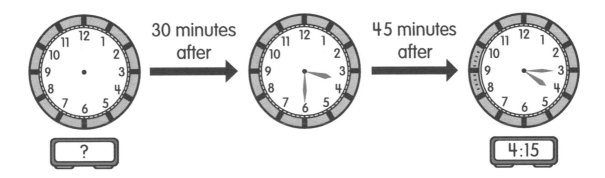

Kent left his house at _____.

PROBLEM SOLVING
Exploration

9. Draw the hands on the clocks to show the time.
Do you see a pattern?
Explain any pattern you find.

12:00

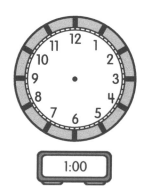

12:30

1:00

1:30

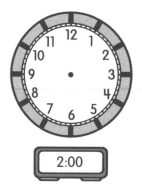

2:00

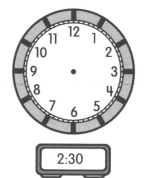

2:30

_____

_____

_____

Name: _____   Date: _____

 **Journal Writing**

Explain.

10. A student writes 8:20 to show the time that is on the clock.
Explain why the student writes the time as 8:20.

_____

_____

_____

_____

_____

11. The teacher asks Milton to draw the hands on the clock to show 7:30.
Milton's clock is shown below.
Is his drawing correct?
Explain.

_____

_____

_____

_____

_____

12. Complete the journal.

Time	What I do at this time.
7:00 A.M.	_____.
8:00 A.M.	_____.
10:00 A.M.	_____.
12:00 P.M.	_____.
1:00 P.M.	_____.
3:00 P.M.	_____.
5:00 P.M.	_____.
6:00 P.M.	_____.
8:00 P.M.	_____.
10:00 P.M.	_____.

Multiplication Tables of 3 and 4

Thinking Skills

Use the numbers to form two multiplication sentences.
Use each number once.

1.

3	4	5	9	20	27

    a.   _____ × _____ = _____

    b.   _____ × _____ = _____

Use the numbers to form two multiplication sentences.
You do not need to use all the numbers.

2.

9	8	24	4	30	27	6	3	20

    a.   _____ × _____ = _____

    b.   _____ × _____ = _____

● **Multiply the ◯s to get the ☐s.**

Fill in the ◯s first.

Then fill in the ☐s.

3.

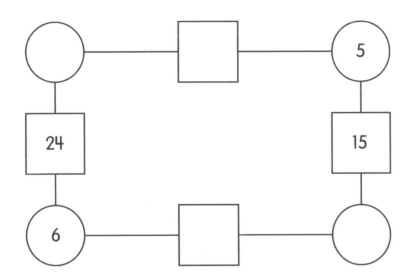

●

Fill in the blanks.

4.   Complete the number pattern.

21, 4, 18, 8, 15, _____, _____

Strategies

One of the three numbers in the box is put into the machine.
The machine produces the final number.

Multiply to fill in the ⬜ s and ◯ s in the machine.

3   6   9

5.

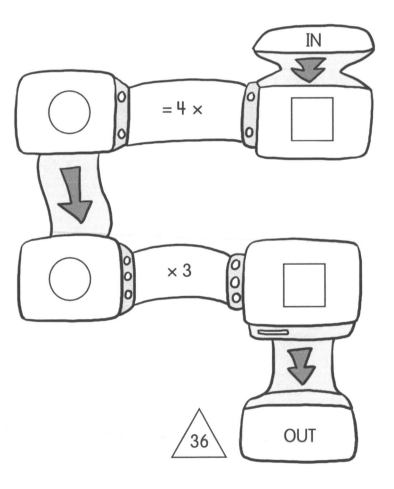

IN

= 4 ×

× 3

36   OUT

Solve
Show your work.

6. A toy train has 8 compartments and an engine
   that is 8 inches long.
   Each compartment is 4 inches long.
   Each compartment is joined by links that are 3 inches long.
   How long is the train?

   The train is _____ inches long.

7. Tyler gave 3 bags of marbles to each of his 3 friends.
   Each bag has 4 marbles in it.
   Tyler has 25 marbles left.
   How many marbles did he have at first?

   Tyler had _____ marbles at first.

PROBLEM SOLVING
Exploration

8. Show at least 2 methods to find 4 × 8.

_____

_____

_____

_____.

9. Study the picture.
Write as many multiplication and division sentences as you can.

_____

_____

_____

_____.

10. Write a division story based on this multiplication story.

There are 4 children at a picnic.
Each child has 6 apples.
How many apples are there in all?

_____

_____

_____

_____.

Find the pattern in the first table and use it to fill in the second table.

11.

5	30
20	15
25	10
5	

3	
	9
15	
3	

Journal Writing

Solve and explain.

12.   18 ÷ 3 = _____

Explain how you get the answer.

_____

_____

_____

_____.

13.   Write a multiplication word problem using these words.
Then solve it.

Darnell	4	6	trays	eggs
each	puts	how	many	in all

_____

_____

_____

_____.

14. Write a division word problem using the following words. Then solve it.

Gregory	$24	3	gives	equally	grandchildren
	grandchild	how	much	get	each

_____

_____

_____

_____.

Using Bar Models: Multiplication and Division

CHAPTER 16

PROBLEM SOLVING

Thinking Skills

Solve.
Use the bar model to help you.

1. Carter has 9 red marbles.
   He has three times as many blue marbles as red marbles.
   Carter packs all his marbles equally in 3 bags.
   How many marbles are in each bag?

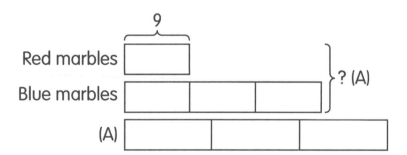

There are _____ marbles in each bag.

Solve.
Use the bar model to help you.

2.   Logan and Seth collect $42 in all.
     Logan collects $15 more than twice as much as Seth.
     How much does Seth collect?

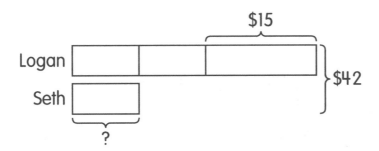

Seth collects $_____.

Study the diagram.
Then find the unknown value of B.

3.

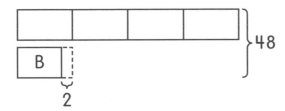

PROBLEM SOLVING
Strategies

Solve.
Use the bar models to help you.
Show your work.

4.   Jasmine has 7 stickers.
Chloe has 4 times as many stickers as Jasmine.
Kim has 15 stickers fewer than Chloe.
How many stickers do they have in all?

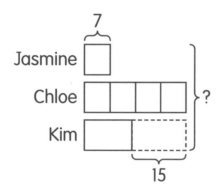

They have _____ stickers in all.

5. Diana has some stamps to give away.
She gives 4 stamps to Peter.
She gives Cody three times as many stamps as she gives Peter.
She gives Timothy half as many stamps as she gives Cody.
Now she has 5 stamps left.
How many stamps did Diana have at first?

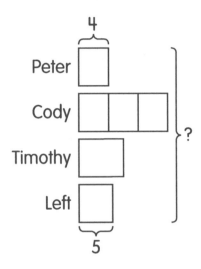

Diana had _____ stamps at first.

Solve.
Draw bar models to help you.
Show your work.

6.   Alexia finds the mass of 3 identical iron cubes and
      5 identical wooden balls.
      The mass of each cube is three times the mass of each ball.
      Each ball has a mass of 3 kilograms.
      What is the total mass of all the cubes and balls?

The total mass of all the cubes and balls is _____ kilograms.

PROBLEM SOLVING
Exploration

Change some parts of the model so that it becomes a model for a multiplication operation.

7.

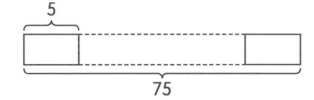

This is a multiplication problem.
Change some words in the problem so that it becomes a division problem.

8.   Kenneth spends $8 for his meal.
Pedro spends 4 times more money than Kenneth spends.
How much money does Pedro spend?

Journal Writing

Study the models.
Write a story problem for each model.
Then solve the problem.

9.

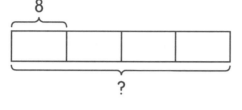

_____

_____

_____

_____ .

10.

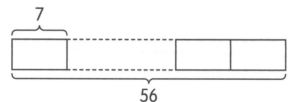

_____

_____

_____

_____ .

CHAPTER 17 Picture Graphs

PROBLEM SOLVING

Thinking Skills

Fill in the blanks.
Use the picture graph to help you.

1. The graph shows the number of books Joel read in 4 months.

Books Read in 4 Months

a. Joel read _____ more books in January and March than in February and April.

b. What is the total number of books that Joel read in February and March? _____

2. The graph shows the number of pancakes sold at a restaurant in a day.

Pancakes Sold in a Day

Banana	◯ ◯ ◯ ◯
Strawberry	◯ ◯ ◯ ◯ ◯ ◯
Butter	◯ ◯ ◯
Chocolate	◯ ◯

Each ◯ stands for 5 pancakes.

a. How many more banana pancakes than chocolate pancakes are sold in a day? _____

b. The total number of _____ pancakes and _____ pancakes sold is the same as the number of strawberry pancakes sold.

3. The table shows the number of ideas presented by each class during the School Innovation Week.

Ideas Presented During School Innovation Week

Class A	△△△△
Class B	△△△△△△△△
Class C	△△△
Class D	△△△△△△
Class E	△△△△

Each △ stands for 3 ideas.

a. How many more ideas were presented by Class B than by Class C? _____

b. Both Class _____ and Class _____ have _____ ideas each.

c. The total number of ideas presented by Class A, C, and E is _____.

Use the given data to complete the picture graph.

Use a ⃝ **to show the items in Ian's collection.**

Put a key under the graph.
Then give the graph a title.

4. a. Ian has 100 items in his collection.

    b. He has 20 pencils in his collection.

    c. He has twice as many erasers as pencils in his collection.

    d. He has 25 stickers in his collection.

    e. The rest of the items in his collection are pens.

Title: _____

Pencils	**Erasers**	**Stickers**	**Pens**

Key: Each ⃝ stands for _____ items.

5. Kelly took a survey in school to find out what color the students like best.

Using the tally chart below, help Kelly
- choose an appropriate key for her graph.
- complete the graph and answer the questions.

Color	Tally	Number of Students
Blue	卌 卌 卌	15
Green	卌 I	6
Red	卌 卌 II	12
Orange	III	3

Title: _____

Blue	Green	Red	Orange

Key: _____.

a. How many students did Kelly include in the survey?

b. How many more students like red than green and orange?

Name: _____   Date: _____

PROBLEM SOLVING
Strategies

Solve.
Use the picture graph to help you.

6. Marie spends 5 days making paper flowers.
    She follows a pattern for the number of flowers she makes
    each day.
    What is the total number of paper flowers she would have made
    by the end of the fifth day?

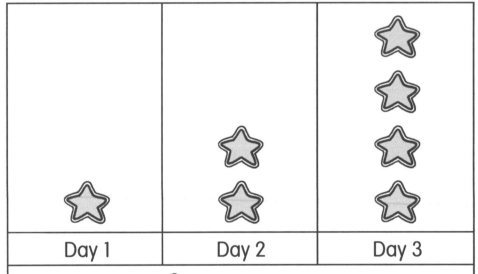

Key: Each stands for 1 paper flower.

Read the data given below.
Put a key under the graph.
Complete the graph.
Give the graph a title.
Then find out how many oranges Hugo bought.

7.   Hugo bought some oranges.
      He gave some of the oranges to his friends.
      He gave Valeria 9 oranges.
      Lenny got 12 more oranges than Valeria.
      Joshua got 6 oranges less than Valeria.
      Hugo had 7 oranges left.

      Title: _____

Lenny	**Valeria**	**Joshua**

      Key: _____

      Hugo bought _____ oranges.

Solve.
Use the picture graphs to help you.

8.   Haley had some marbles.

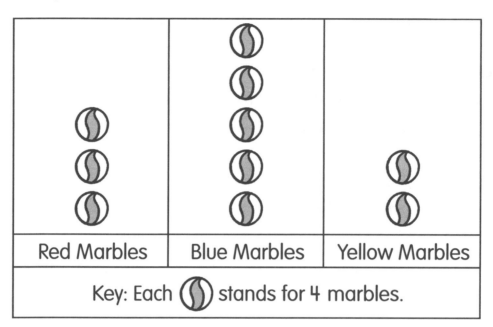

After trading some of his marbles with his friends, he had:

a.   Did Haley have the same number of marbles before and after trading with his friends? _____

b. How many more yellow marbles did Haley have in the end than when he began?

c. How many more blue marbles did Haley have at first than yellow marbles in the end?

PROBLEM SOLVING
Exploration

Solve.
Show your work.
Then complete the picture graph.

9. The graph shows the number of students absent from class last week.
    The total number of students absent on Tuesday and Wednesday is less than the total number of students absent on Monday and Thursday.
    The total number of students absent on Wednesday is more than those absent on Thursday.
    How many students are absent on Tuesday?
    How many students are absent on Wednesday?

Title: _____

Monday	X X X X X X X X
Tuesday	
Wednesday	
Thursday	X X X X
Friday	X X X X X X X X X X
Key: Each **X** stands for 1 student.	

Journal Writing

Solve.
Explain your answer.

10. Look at the picture graph.

The 🩶 stands for 1 piece of fruit.

The third tree has 32 pieces of fruit on it.

The first tree has only 8 pieces of fruit.

How many 🩶 must be drawn for the first tree?

First Tree	Second Tree	Third Tree
	🩶 🩶 🩶	🩶 🩶 🩶 🩶

_____

_____

_____

_____.

Draw a picture graph to help you tell the story.

11.   You have grown some balsam plants.
        These plants have flowers and seeds on them.
        You want to tell a story to your class about the flowers and
        seeds on your plants.

Using your graph, write four sentences about the flowers and
seeds on your plants.
Use some of the words below in your sentences.

(more than   less than   how many   flowers   seeds)

_____

_____

_____

_____.

Name: _____   Date: _____

CHAPTER 18 — Lines and Surfaces

Thinking Skills

Study the letters and numbers carefully.

1. Circle the letter and the number that have 2 parts of lines and 1 curve.

W	5	C	J	E
O	H	S	M	N
X	7	D	3	G

2.

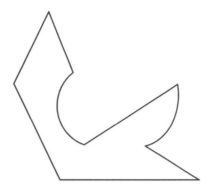

The figure has _____ more parts of lines than curves.

3. Count the number of flat and curved surfaces that these solids have.

Solid	Flat Surface	Curved Surface

How many more flat surfaces does the cube have than the

sphere has curved surfaces? _____

4.   Count the number of parts of lines and curves of the solid.

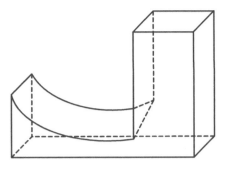

Parts of lines _____

Curves _____

5.   Look at the pictures.
Use them to answer the questions.

   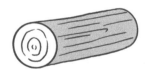   

tissue box   log   chocolate bar   soccer ball

a.   I have both flat and curved surfaces. What am I?

_____

b.   I have 2 flat surfaces less than a solid cube.
I can slide but I cannot stack.
What am I?

_____

PROBLEM SOLVING

Strategies

Solve
Show your work.

6. Peter is given two types of solid objects.
   Each Object A has 4 flat surfaces.
   Each Object B has 2 flat surfaces and 2 curved surfaces.
   There are a total of 36 flat surfaces and 8 curved surfaces in all
   the objects Peter is given.
   How many of each object is Peter given?

7. Evan has 6 solid shapes, some of Shape A and some of Shape B.
   There are 33 flat surfaces in all.
   How many of each solid shape does Evan have?

Shape A   Shape B

Name: _____   Date: _____

PROBLEM SOLVING
Exploration

8.   Count the number of flat surfaces and corners of the cube and
        rectangular prism.
        Record them in the table.

	Cube	Rectangular Prism
Flat Surfaces		
Corners		

     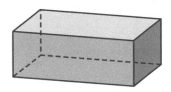

          cube   rectangular prism

What do these numbers tell you about the flat surfaces and
corners of a cube and a rectangular prism?
Describe.

_____

_____

_____

_____

9. Count the number of flat surfaces and corners of the pyramids. Record them in the table.

	Pyramid A	Pyramid B
Flat Surfaces		
Corners		

Pyramid A

Pyramid B

What do these numbers tell you about the flat surfaces and corners of pyramids?
Describe.

_____

_____

_____

_____.

Journal Writing

10. Look at the object.
    Write a story about the object using some of the words in the box.

parts of a line	curves	flat surfaces
curved surfaces	stack	roll

_____

_____

_____

_____.

Shapes and Patterns

PROBLEM SOLVING
Thinking Skills

Draw lines on the figure to show how it is formed from 2 semicircles, a triangle, and a rectangle.

1.

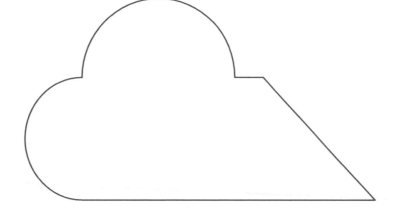

This is a semicircle.

● **Look at the picture.**
Then answer the questions.

2.   The box contains 5 shapes.

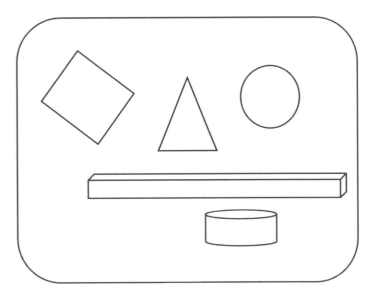

a.   How many shapes will there be in 4 identical boxes?

b.   How many more shapes must you put into each of the
     4 boxes so that the total number of shapes is 32?

3. Color the rectangles red, the squares orange, the triangles yellow, and the circles green.

How many more circles than squares are there in the figure?

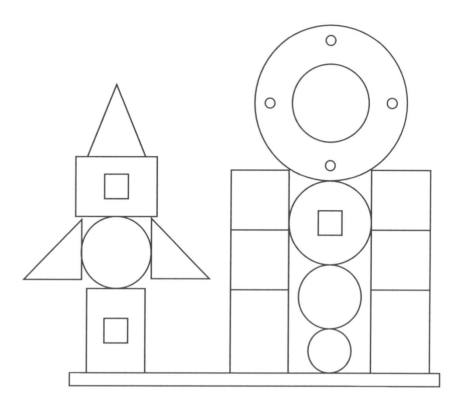

4. The model is made up of bricks laid in a pattern.
How many more pieces of bricks are needed to complete the model of a rectangular wall?

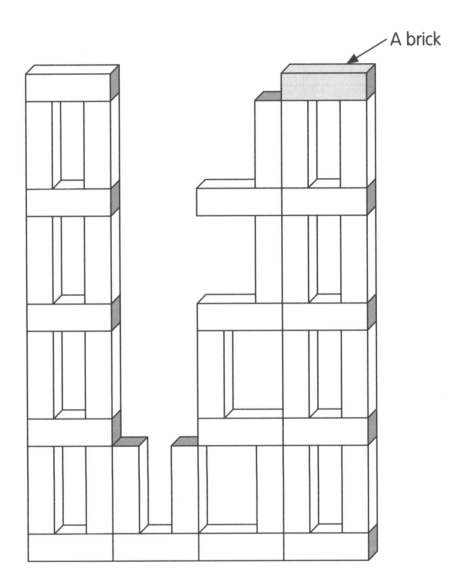

A brick

5. The picture shows shapes placed in a pattern.
Circle the shapes that are placed incorrectly.

PROBLEM SOLVING
Strategies

Circle the shape that comes next in the pattern.

6.

   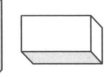 ?

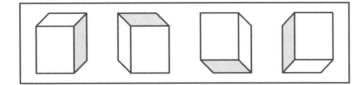

Study the pattern carefully.
How many squares will be in figure P4?

7.

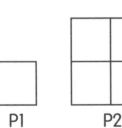 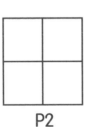 

P1   P2   P3

1   4   9

Name: _____ Date: _____

PROBLEM SOLVING

Exploration

Draw 2 sets of patterns using any three of these shapes.

8.

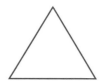   

Journal Writing

Describe each pattern.

9.

_____

_____

_____

_____ .

10.

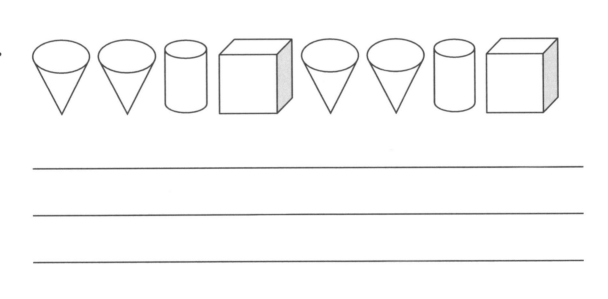

_____

_____

_____

_____ .

Answers

Chapter 10

1. Thinking Skill: Analyzing parts and whole
   Solution: 217 − 90 = <u>127</u>

2. Thinking Skill: Comparing
   Solution:
   195 + 5 = 200
   645 − 200 = 445

3. 30 + 60 = 90

4. $17 + $17 + $8 + $8 + $8
   Estimate to the nearest 10:
   $20 + $20 + $10 + $10 + $10 = $70

5. Strategy: Use a diagram
   Solution:

   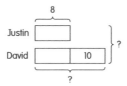

   8 + 10 = 18
   18 + 8 = 26

6. $17 − $8 = $9
   Estimate to the nearest 10
   $20 + $10 = $30

7. Strategy: Work backward
   Solution:
   25 + 60 + 30 = 115 pages

8. Strategy: Use before-and-after concept
   Solution:
   Now: 10 apples
              10 oranges
   Before: 10 + 8 = 18
              10 − 7 = 3
   18 + 3 = 21 apples and oranges

9. Strategy: Look for patterns
   Solution:
   Identify the pattern of
   115 − 114, 113 − 112, 111 − 110, 109 − 108,
   Each equals 1.
   So, 1 + 1 + 1 + 1 = 4.

10. **Method 1**
    160 + 100 = 260
    260 − 20 = 240

    Method 2
    200 + 80 = 280
    280 − 40 = 240

11. **Method 1**
    540 − 100 = 440
    440 + 30 = 470

    Method 2
    600 − 100 = 500
    60 − 30 = 30
    500 − 30 = 470

12. **Step 1:** First add 10 to 137 = 147
    Step 2: Now subtract 2 from 147 = 145

13. **Step 1:** First add 10 to 129 = 139
    Step 2: Now subtract 3 from 139 = 136

14. **Step 1:** First subtract 10 from 234 = 224
    Step 2: Now add 4 to 224 = 228

15. **Step 1:** First subtract 10 from 462 = 452
    Step 2: Now add 1 to 452 = 453

16. The greatest numbers that can be rounded to
    80 are: 81, 82, 83, and 84.
    The least numbers that can be rounded to 80
    are: 75, 76, 77, 78 and 79.

17. The greatest numbers that can be rounded to
    460 are: 461, 462, 463, and 464.
    The least numbers that can be rounded to
    460 are: 455, 456, 457, 458 and 459.

Chapter 11

1. Thinking Skill: Comparing
   Solution:
   $7 + $5 + $3 = $15
   Ethan can buy <u>cheese, sardines, and butter</u>.

2. Thinking Skill: Analyzing parts and whole
   Solution:
   $103 − $26 − $17 − $7 = $53
   The watch cost $<u>53</u>.

3. Strategy: Look for patterns
   Solution:

4. Strategy: Use a diagram
   Solution:

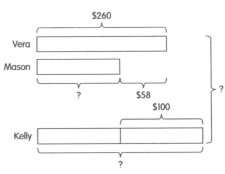

$260 − $58 = $202
Mason saved $202.
$202 + $100 = $302
Kelly saved $302.
$260 + $202 + $302 = $764
They saved $764 in all.

5.

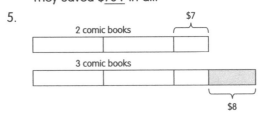

$7 + $8 = $15
Each comic book costs $15.

6. Strategy: Use a diagram
   Solution:

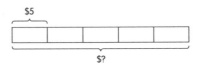

$5 + $5 + $5 + $5 + $5 = $25
Jacob spent $25.

7. Strategy: Use a diagram
   Solution: $11 + $11 = $22
   $22 + $3 = $25
   Eugene spent $25.

8. Strategy: Use guess and check
   Solution:

   ◯ + ☐ + ☐ = $450 -- A

   ◯ + ◯ + ☐ = $300 -- B

◯	☐	A	B	Is the answer correct?
50	50	150	150	no
100	50	200	250	no
200	50	300	450	no
50	200	450	300	yes

   ◯ = $50.

9. Answers vary.
   Sample answer:
   $10 + $5 + $1 + $1 + $1 + $1 + $1 = $20
   $5 + $5 + $5 + $5 = $20
   $10 + $10 = $20

10. a. $2.25 + $2.50 + $1.50 + $3.00 = $9.25
    Caroline can buy a vase, a pack of
    envelopes, a pencil case, and a teddy bear.
    b. $6 + $3 = $9
    Caroline can buy a book and a teddy bear.

11. Answers vary.
    Sample answer:
    Step 1: Compare the dollars first. They are
    the same.

    Step 2: Compare the cents. 65 is greater
    than 30.

    So, $45.30 is less than $45.65.

12. Answers vary.
    Sample answer:
    Ryan has $550.
    He buys a new suit.
    He has $192 left.
    How much does the new suit cost?

Chapter 12

1. Thinking skill: Analyzing parts and whole
   Solution:

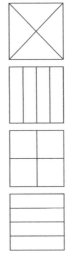

© Marshall Cavendish International (Singapore) Private Limited.

2. Thinking skill: Analyzing parts and whole
   Solution:

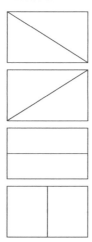

3. Thinking skills: Comparing, Sequencing
   Solution:

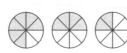

4. Thinking skills: Comparing, Sequencing
   Solution:

5. Thinking skills: Comparing, Sequencing
   Solution:

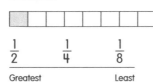

   $\frac{1}{2}$ $\frac{1}{4}$ $\frac{1}{8}$

   Greatest   Least

6. Thinking skills: Comparing, Sequencing
   Solution:

   $\frac{6}{8}, \frac{4}{8}, \frac{2}{8}$

7. Thinking skill: Analyzing parts and whole
   Solution:
   Assume pizza is 1 whole.
   Then,
   $$1 - \frac{2}{9} - \frac{4}{9} = \frac{3}{9} = \frac{1}{3}$$
   Sydney eats $\frac{1}{3}$ of the pizza.

8. Strategy: Look for patterns
   Solution:
   $\frac{6}{9}$ or $\frac{2}{3}$

9. Strategy: Work backward
   Solution:
   $5 + 2 + 3 + 2 = 12$
   So, the fraction of crayons left $= \frac{2}{12} = \frac{1}{6}$
   Calvin has $\frac{1}{6}$ of the crayons left.

10. Strategy: Use a diagram
    Solution:

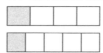

    Ava

    Hailey

    $$\frac{11}{12} - \frac{5}{12} = \frac{6}{12} = \frac{1}{2}$$
    Ava must give $\frac{5}{12}$ of the bread to Hailey.

11. Each fraction shows the amount you get by cutting the previous fraction into two equal parts.

12. $\frac{1}{6}, \frac{1}{12}, \frac{1}{24}$

13. We can show the fraction in the bar form.

    As we see in the bar $\frac{1}{5}$ is less than $\frac{1}{4}$.

14.

    $\frac{1}{2}$ of $\frac{5}{6}$ will be $\frac{5}{6} \times \frac{1}{2} = \frac{5}{12}$

Chapter 13

1. Thinking skill: Comparing
   Solution:
   $87 - 49 = 38$ inches;
   $49 - 38 = 11$ inches
   Kenny jumped 11 inches farther than Jim.

2. Thinking skill: Comparing
   Solution:
   $19 + 12 + 7 = 38$ inches

3. Thinking skill: Comparing
   Solution: 5

4. Thinking skill: Comparing
   Solution: A

5. Thinking skill: Comparing
   Solution: 1

6. Thinking skill: Analyzing parts and whole
   Solution: 9

7. Strategy: Look for patterns
   Solution:
   12 ft; 96 ft
   Number plus itself, gives next number to form
   a pattern
   Example:
   $3 + 3 = 6$
   $6 + 6 = 12$
   $12 + 12 = 24$; $24 + 24 = 48$;
   $48 + 48 = 96$; $96 + 96 = 192$

8. Strategy: Use a diagram
   Solution:
   Each pole is $= 3$ ft $+ 2$ ft $+ 3$ ft $+ 2$ ft
   $\qquad\qquad = 10$ ft
   $10 \times 7 = 70$ ft
   The line of pole is <u>70</u> feet long.

9. Strategy: Use a diagram
   Solution:

   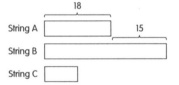

   $18 + 15 = 33$ inches (String B)
   $18 \div 2 = 9$ inches (String C)
   $33 + 9 = 42$ inches (String B and C)

   The total Length of String B and String C is
   <u>42</u> inches.

10. Strategy: Work backward
    Solution:
    $18 + 6 + 25 + 7 = 56$ ft
    Grandma Lucille bought <u>56</u> feet of cloth.

11. Answers vary.

12. Answers vary.

13. **Step 1:** Read the marking on the ruler where
    the pencil ends: 8 inches.
    Step 2: Subtract to find the length of the pencil:
    $8 - 2 = 6$
    The pencil is 6 inches long.

14. Answers vary.
    Sample answer:
    Mike is 95 inches tall.
    Larry is twice as tall as Mike.
    Melvin is 5 inches taller than Larry.
    Find the height of the tallest boy.

Chapter 14

1. Thinking skill: Comparing
   Solution: 4:55

2. Thinking skill: Comparing
   Solution:

   4:30 P.M.

3. Thinking skill: Comparing
   Solution:

   6:35 P.M.

4. Thinking skill: Comparing
   Solution:

   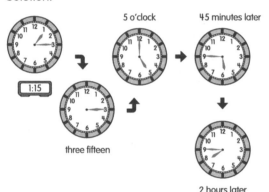

5. Strategy: Look for patterns
   Solution:

6. Strategy: Simplify the problem
   Solution: 20 min

   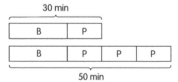

   3 posters + 1 banner = 50 min
   1 poster + 1 banner = 30 min
   2 posters = $50 - 30 = 20$ min
   1 poster = 10 min
   1 banner = $30 - 10 = 20$ min

   It takes <u>20</u> minutes to print a banner.

7. Strategy: Use a diagram

Solution:

$36 - 28 = 8$
$8 \times 2 = 16$ min

Sandy took <u>16</u> minutes to draw a picture.

8. Strategy: Work backward

Solution: 3:00 P.M.

Kent left his house at 3:00 P.M.

9. When the minute hand moves from 12 to 6 the hour hand moves to half way between the hours. When the minute hand goes up to 12 again, the hour hand moves to the next hour.

10. The student writes the time as 8:20 because the minute hand is at 4 and the hour hand is slightly past 8.

11. 7:30 incorrectly shown. The hour hand should be between 7 and 8.

12. Answers vary.

Chapter 15

1. Thinking skills: Deduction, Analyzing parts and whole

Solution:
a. $4 \times 5 = 20$
b. $3 \times 9 = 27$

2. Strategy: Use guess and check

Solution:
a. $9 \times 3 = 27$
b. $4 \times 6 = 24$

3. Thinking skill: Identifying patterns and relationships

Solution:

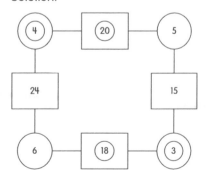

4. Strategy: Look for patterns

Solution: The pattern is in decreasing as well as increasing order.
21; 18; 15 in the decreasing order the next number is 12.
4; 8 in the increasing order the next number is 12.
12; 12

5. Thinking skill: Deduction

Solution: 3

6. Strategy: Look for patterns

Solution:

$4 \times 8 = 32$
$8 \times 3 = 24$
$8 + 24 + 32 = 64$ in.

The train is <u>64</u> inches long.

7. Strategy: Work backward

Solution:
$3 \times 3 = 9$
$9 \times 4 = 36$
$36 + 25 = 61$

Tyler had <u>61</u> marbles at first.

8. Answers vary.
Sample answer:
Method 1: $4 + 4 + 4 + 4 + 4 + 4 + 4 + 4 = 32$

Method 2: $4 \times 5 + 4 \times 3$
$20 + 12 = 32$

9. $4 \times 5 = 20$ $20 \div 5 = 4$
$5 \times 4 = 20$ $20 \div 4 = 5$

10. Expected Answer:
4 children bring a total of 24 apples to a picnic. Each child brings an equal number of apples. How many apples does each child bring?

11. Thinking skill: Identifying patterns and relationships

Solution:
Pattern in the first table: The numbers in each row add up to 35, or 7 times the bottom number.

5	30
20	15
25	10
5	

3	(18)
(12)	9
15	(6)
3	

© Marshall Cavendish International (Singapore) Private Limited.

12. Expected answer:
    Use related multiplication facts.
    $3 \times 6 = 18$, so 18 divided by 3 is 6.

13. Sample answer:
    Darnell has 4 trays.
    He puts 6 eggs on each tray.
    How many eggs does he have in all?
    $4 \times 6 = 24$

14. Sample answer:
    Gregory has $24.
    He gives the money equally to his 3 grandchildren.
    How much does each grandchild get?
    $24 \div 3 = 8

Chapter 16

1. Thinking skill: Analyzing parts and whole
   Solution:
   Red = 9
   Blue = $9 \times 3 = 27$
   $27 + 9 = 36$
   $36 \div 3 = 12$

   There are 12 marbles in each bag.

2. Thinking skill: Comparing
   Solution:
   $42 - $15 = 27
   $27 \div $3 = 9

   Seth collects $9.

3. Thinking skill: Analyzing parts and whole
   Solution:
   $48 + 2 = 50$
   $50 \div 5 = 10$
   $B = 10 - 2 = 8$

4. Strategy: Use a diagram
   Solution:
   $7 \times 4 = 28$
   $28 - 15 = 13$
   $7 + 28 + 13 = 48$

   They have 48 stickers in all.

5. Strategy: Use a diagram
   Solution:
   $P \longrightarrow 4$
   $C \longrightarrow 4 \times 3 = 12$
   $T \longrightarrow 12 \div 2 = 6$
   Left $\longrightarrow 5$
   At first = $5 + 6 + 12 + 4 = 27$

   Diana had 27 stamps at first.

6. Strategy: Use a diagram
   Solution:

   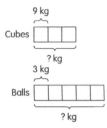

   $3 \times 3 = 9$ (mass of 1 cube)
   $9 \times 3 = 27$
   $5 \times 3 = 15$
   $15 + 27 = 42$ kg

   The total mass of all the cubes and balls is 42 kilograms.

7.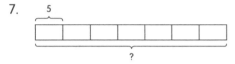

8. Expected Answer:
   Kenneth and Pedro spend a total of $48 for their meals.
   Pedro spends 4 times more money than Kenneth spends.
   How much does Kenneth spend?

9. Answers vary.
   Sample answer:
   Robin gives an equal number of crackers to 4 friends.
   He gives 8 crackers to Sam.
   How many crackers does he give in all?
   $8 \times 4 = 32$

10. Answers vary.
    Sample answer:
    Mr. Simon gives away 56 crayons in all.
    He gives 7 crayons to each student.
    How many students are there in all?
    $56 \div 7 = 8$

Chapter 17

1. Thinking skill: Comparing
   Solution:
   a. 6
   b. 18

2. Thinking skill: Comparing
   Solution:
   a. 10
   b. banana; chocolate

3. Thinking skill: Comparing
Solution:
a. 15
b. A, E, 12
c. 33

4. Thinking skill: Deduction
Solution:
Title: Items in Ian's Collection

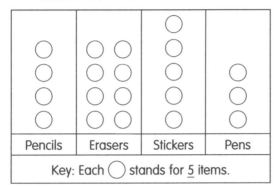

Pencils	Erasers	Stickers	Pens

Key: Each ◯ stands for 5 items.

Recommended scale is 5 items per ◯ since data are multiples of 5.

5. Thinking skill: Deduction
Solution:
Title: Color Students Like

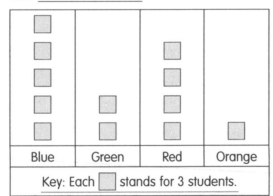

Blue	Green	Red	Orange

Key: Each ☐ stands for 3 students.

a. 15 + 6 + 12 + 3 = 36
b. 12 – 6 – 3 = 3
Recommended scale is 3 students per ☐ since responses are all multiples of 3.

6. Strategy: Look for patterns
Solution:
Marie doubles the number of flowers she makes each day.
First day: 1
Second day: 1 + 1 = 2
Third day: 2 + 2 = 4
Fourth day: 4 + 4 = 8
Fifth day: 8 + 8 = 16
So after the fifth day she has:
1 + 2 + 4 + 8 + 16 = 31
Or

Marie increases the number of additional flowers she makes each day by one.
First day: 1
Second day: 1 + 1 = 2
Third day: 2 + 2 = 4
Fourth day: 4 + 3 = 7
Fifth day: 7 + 4 = 11
So after the fifth day she has:
1 + 2 + 4 + 7 + 11 = 25

7. Strategy: Work backward
Solution:
Title: Number of Oranges Hugo Gave Away

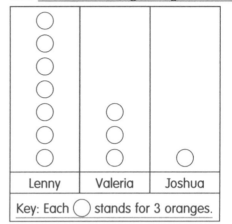

Lenny	Valeria	Joshua

Key: Each ◯ stands for 3 oranges.

Recommended scale is 3 oranges per ◯ since data are multiples of 3.
Valeria ⟶ 9
Lenny ⟶ 12 + 9 = 21
Joshua ⟶ 9 – 6 = 3
Hugo ⟶ 9 + 21 + 3 + 7 = 40

Hugo bought 40 oranges.

8. Strategy: Use before-and-after concept
Solution:
a. No; b. 8; c. 4

9. Answers vary.
The total number of students absent on Tuesday and Wednesday is less than 12.
The possible answers are:
Wed: 5; 6; 7; 8; 9; 10; 11
Tue: 0; 1; 2; 3; 4
The total of these numbers is less than 12:

5 + 0 = 5	6 + 4 = 10	8 + 3 = 11
5 + 1 = 6	7 + 0 = 7	9 + 0 = 9
5 + 2 = 7	7 + 1 = 8	9 + 1 = 10
5 + 3 = 8	7 + 2 = 9	9 + 2 = 11
5 + 4 = 9	7 + 3 = 10	10 + 0 = 10
6 + 0 = 6	7 + 4 = 11	10 + 1 = 11
6 + 1 = 7	8 + 0 = 8	11 + 0 = 11
6 + 2 = 8	8 + 1 = 9	
6 + 3 = 9	8 + 2 = 10	

10. The third tree has 32 pieces of fruit represented
    by 4 pictures.
    $32 ÷ 4 = 8$
    So, each picture represents 8 pieces of fruit.
    The second tree has 3 pictures so the tree has
    24 pieces of fruit.
    $8 × 3 = 24$
    The first tree has 8 pieces of fruit. So, only
    1 picture will be drawn.

11. Answers vary.
    Sample answer:

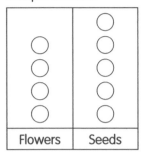

Flowers	Seeds

There are 20 flowers in the garden.
There are more seeds than flowers.
The number of seeds is less than 30.
How many flowers and seeds are there?

Chapter 18

1. Thinking skill: Comparing
   Solution: 5; G

2. Thinking skill: Comparing
   Solution: 4

3. Thinking skill: Classifying
   Solution:

Solid	Flat Surface	Curved Surface
	6	0
	0	1
	2	1

$6 - 1 = 5$

4. Thinking skill: Classifying
   Solution:
   16 (5 hidden) parts of lines
   2 curves

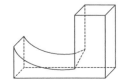

5. Thinking skill: Classifying
   Solution:
   a. log
   b. chocolate bar

6. Strategy: Simplify the problem
   Solution:
   Curved objects: $8 ÷ 2 = 4$ (Object B)
   Flat surfaces: $36 - 8 = 28$
   $28 ÷ 4 = 7$ (Object A)

7. Strategies: Make suppositions, Make a
                systematic list
   Solution:
   A – 6 flat surfaces
   B – 5 flat surfaces
   Assuming all are of shape B.
   5   5   5   5   5   5
           (total 30)
   So some must be of shape A.
   6   6   6   5   5   5
           (total 33)
   So, Evan had 3 solids that are of shape A and
   3 solids that are of shape B.

8.

	Cube	Rectangular prism
flat surfaces	6	6
corners	8	8

The number of corners is more than the
number of flat surfaces in a cube and a
rectangular prism.
Or
A cube and a rectangular prism have the same
number of flat surfaces. They also have the
same number of corners.

9.

	Pyramid A	Pyramid B
flat surfaces	5	4
corners	5	4

The number of flat surfaces and the number of
corners are the same in pyramids.

10. Answers vary.

Chapter 19

1. Thinking skill: Identifying patterns and relationships

    Solution:

    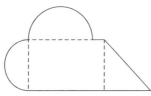

2. Thinking skills: Comparing, Analyzing parts and whole

    Solution: a. 20; b. 3

3. Thinking skills: Classifying, Comparing

    Solution:
    Rectangles: 5 or 12 (including squares)
    Triangles: 3
    Squares: 7
    Circles: 10
    $10 - 7 = 3$

4. Thinking skills: Identifying patterns and relationships, Comparing, Spatial visualization

    Solution:

    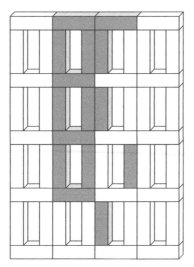

    15 more pieces of bricks

5. Thinking skill: Identifying patterns and relationships

6. Strategy: Look for patterns
    Solution:

7. Strategy: Look for patterns
    Solution:

    Patttern 4 = 16

8. Answers vary.
9. Answers vary.
10. Answers vary.